John Adams

BARNES & NOBLE® READER'S COMPANION™
Today's take on tomorrow's classics.

FICTION
THE CORRECTIONS by Jonathan Franzen
I KNOW WHY THE CAGED BIRD SINGS by Maya Angelou
THE JOY LUCK CLUB by Amy Tan
THE LOVELY BONES by Alice Sebold
THE POISONWOOD BIBLE by Barbara Kingsolver
THE RED TENT by Anita Diamant
WE WERE THE MULVANEYS by Joyce Carol Oates
WHITE TEETH by Zadie Smith

NONFICTION
THE ART OF WAR by Sun Tzu
A BRIEF HISTORY OF TIME by Stephen Hawking
GUNS, GERMS, AND STEEL by Jared Diamond
JOHN ADAMS by David McCullough

DAVID McCULLOUGH'S

John Adams

BARNES
&NOBLE
B O O K S

EDITORIAL DIRECTOR Justin Kestler
EXECUTIVE EDITOR Ben Florman
DIRECTOR OF TECHNOLOGY Tammy Hepps

SERIES EDITOR John Crowther
MANAGING EDITOR Vincent Janoski

WRITER John Henriksen
EDITOR Matt Blanchard
DESIGN Dan O. Williams, Matt Daniels

This edition published by Spark Publishing

Spark Publishing
A Division of SparkNotes LLC
120 Fifth Avenue, 8th Floor
New York, NY 10011

ISBN 1-58663-865-3

Library of Congress Cataloging-in-Publication Data available upon request

Printed and bound in the United States

Contents

A TOUR OF THE BOOK an overview of the book **1**

The Founding Stepfather *John Adams* rescues our second president from the dustbin of history, providing great new insight into a largely forgotten man.

JOURNEYS the Founding Fathers and their stories **11**

The Supporting Players Adams was a key figure among our nation's founders—but has been overshadowed by some of his more colorful counterparts.

POINTS OF VIEW a conversation about *John Adams* **23**

A President But No Politician Adams's unglamorous, no-nonsense style would likely have made him an ugly duckling in the media circus of today's politics.

A WRITER'S LIFE David McCullough's story **43**

From Pittsburgh to the Pulitzer The prolific David McCullough is one of today's most popular and acclaimed retellers of our American past.

THE WORLD OUTSIDE a look at colonial America **47**

The New Kid on the Block In Adams's time, America was seen—and frequently mocked—as a remote, backward outpost of little importance.

A BRIEF HISTORY the critics respond to *John Adams* **53**

A Reputation Restored In John Adams, McCullough revisited what many considered a boring subject and turned it into a runaway bestseller.

EXPLORE books to consider reading next **57**

Other Books of Interest John Adams isn't the first of McCullough's successes—or the first bestselling biography of a Founding Father.

John Adams

The Founding Stepfather

John Adams rescues our second president from the dustbin of history, providing great new insight into a largely forgotten man.

HOW CAN THE BIOGRAPHY of a somewhat forgotten American patriot and president, active more than two centuries ago, land on the *New York Times* bestseller list and stay there for more than a year? The answer partly lies in the skill of the author, historian David McCullough, in bringing out the fascinating side of his subject. His straightforward, easy-to-read biography balances the personal and the public to give us a full picture of Adams and his times. We finish *John Adams* feeling as familiar with Adams's daughter's marital problems as with the difficulties of establishing trade agreements with France. We learn as much about Thomas Jefferson's shopping habits as we do about foreign relations in 1798. McCullough has a brilliant knack for merging the hard facts of diplomatic and military history with softer material about everyday life. Rather than clobber us with abstract historical speculations, he introduces us to a stage full of vibrant individuals who shape history before our eyes. The result is a highly personal and engaging approach to a period that many of us know less about than we are willing to admit.

But the popularity of McCullough's biography is due to more than the author's skills. Like other great works of history, *John Adams* provides not only the facts, but also ways to connect past with present—ways to allow the past to give meaning to today's world. Published only months before the national trauma of September 11, 2001, *John Adams* is a reflection not just on one man, but on the meaning of the United States. It reaches back to America's origins, allowing us to explore what it meant to be an American and to serve one's country in the nation's important early days.

Heroic struggle and dazzling leadership are only part of the picture McCullough paints of postrevolutionary America. There was a drearier side to serving the nation too—long hours of drudgery, working endlessly behind the scenes for little public credit, sacrificing family life for the good of the country, and dealing with journalistic slurs and the attacks of enemies. Adams was the first U.S. president who had to deal with the media on a regular basis—his predecessor, George Washington, never dealt with such a relentlessly antagonistic press. Adams didn't have the luxury of "spin doctors" or teams of public relations experts who could soften the blows of the media. Adams was largely on his own, looking around in perplexity at what the world said about him. In large part, this uncomfortable public exposure was what holding office entailed for John Adams—all at a salary that hardly allowed him to support his household.

"Adams was not a man of the world. He enjoyed no social standing. He was an awkward dancer and poor at cards. He never learned to flatter."

Such a dismal image of Adams's patriotic service in early America may come as something of a surprise to those of us brought up on the standard grade-school picture of American history. It's at odds with our grand and spectacular images of Washington crossing the Delaware and American riflemen firing at British redcoats. Adams didn't become the stuff of legend. Poets didn't write ballads about him as they did of Paul Revere. Adams didn't pass into American folklore—children don't tell stories about John Adams chopping down a cherry tree and saying he couldn't tell a lie.

But lack of glamour may be precisely the reason why Adams's life appears so attractive today. Part of the appeal of the man we see in *John Adams* might be due to the fact that he *isn't* the textbook image of a national hero. In our time, when Hollywood satires of Washington politicians are rampant and Americans more skeptical than ever before of the media's influence on democracy, Adams's relative ordinariness, in contrast to his political contemporaries' privilege and flashiness, makes him seem believable and real. What some historians have read as blandness is actually a down-to-earth authenticity. Ironically, Adams may have been as preoccupied with his image as many modern media stars are: many of his contemporaries accused him of being vain and too interested in his own reputation.

Even so, McCullough portrays Adams as an individual well aware that the noble task of starting a new government demanded a vast amount of unavoidable grunt work. The realism and humility of such an attitude is admirable, especially in the context of the media-circus political environment of our own times.

PERSONAL SACRIFICES

Adams's personal life bears the marks of the sacrifices he made for his country. When Adams was elected as one of the Massachusetts delegates to the Continental Congress before the Revolution, he gave up a thriving practice as a traveling lawyer and the hefty salary that went with it. His new post subjected him and his family to a lifetime of meager official salaries that just barely supported the household—for Adams was not independently wealthy. As McCullough tells us, Adams was dismayed to see that yokels back in his hometown were making huge fortunes while he was paid so meagerly. The family continuously felt financially pinched, and at times they were in dire straits. McCullough's book opens with a plea to Adams from his wife, Abigail, to buy pins on his trip—not to use for sewing, but to trade for other domestic necessities. Adams's independently wealthy political colleagues could bear the tiny official salaries far better than he could: George Washington and Benjamin Franklin were two of the richest men in the country, and Thomas Jefferson threw around money recklessly (though his finances were messy). When Adams was appointed as the nation's first ambassador to England, he fretted over the expenses the post demanded. When the federal government moved to New York City, one of Adams's main concerns was how he would support his family in such an expensive place. Even as president in the new capital of Washington, D.C., life wasn't cushy. The newly built White House was impressive, but it was barely furnished and had empty walls and a shortage of servant staff.

McCullough's focus on these financial worries makes Adams a sympathetic figure, an everyday man many of us can relate to in his struggle to make ends meet. Washington and Jefferson believed that public officials should receive no salary at all in order to attract only high-minded candidates. But Adams believed the presidency was a job like any other and that it should be compensated accordingly. To Adams, the president wasn't a superstar, but a normal man with work to do. Today, Adams's down-to-earth views about money and professionalism make him seem more contemporary to us than many of his aristocratic associates.

On top of financial strain, Adams was frustrated by the lack of time he could devote to his family—another hardship that strikes a chord with many modern readers. Abigail was particularly burdened by Adams's career, putting up with his absence from home for years. When Adams was chosen as an American envoy to the French court, he decided to sail to France without Abigail. Later, when Adams served as vice president in the national capital of Philadelphia, he had Abigail stay at home in Massachusetts because he feared she would fall ill with the malaria that ran rampant in the capital. She put up with the extended absences bravely, but her letters clearly indicate that she eventually got fed up with their long-distance marriage. "All things look gloomy and melancholy around me," she wrote to him in France in 1778. "You could not have suffered more upon your voyage than I have felt cut off from all communication with you." Abigail's complaint seems justified—in six months she received only two letters from her husband. He claimed that as many as fifty got lost in the mail, but it's more likely that his duties in France overwhelmed him and that Congress's failure to recognize his service depressed him. In any case, it's clear that Adams's official work got in the

Domestic tranquility

Adams was the first president to live in the White House, moving in with Abigail in November 1800. In its early months, the official residence was hardly the lap of luxury we know today. The Adamses moved in to find the paint still wet, the roof unfinished, and the house desperately understaffed. Abigail did the family's laundry herself, hanging it to dry in the East Room—a place now more appropriately used for receptions, official dinners, press conferences, and bill-signing ceremonies.

way of his marriage and that he could do little about it. He wrote back to Abigail somewhat bitterly, "For God's sake, never reproach me again with not writing. . . . You know not—you feel not—the dangers that surround me, nor those that may be brought upon our country."

Adams also worried about his distance from his children—later, he claimed they were responsible for turning his hair gray. Adams's daughter, Nabby, married a rogue. His son, Charles, constantly got into trouble, from his student days when he ran naked through Harvard Yard until his later years when he became an alcoholic and went bankrupt. Adams made every effort to visit both children whenever possible, though he eventually announced his intention to renounce Charles. Still, life in Washington, D.C., made huge claims upon Adams, and he could seldom get away.

We tend not to associate everyday family concerns with larger-than-life presidents like George Washington or Abraham Lincoln. McCullough's biography is a reminder that presidents can be ordinary individuals with ordinary problems as much as they can be larger-than-life figures. His portrayal of Adams resists idealizing the presidency by reminding us of the human limitations that even presidents must confront. Washington may have been the first American superstar, but McCullough shows us that Adams was in many ways an ordinary man with ordinary problems who happened to hold high public office.

A POLITICAL GUINEA PIG

In addition to his personal sacrifices, Adams also faced political quandaries that his predecessor never did. George Washington led a relatively blissful existence as head of the nation. He had an almost universally adoring public at his beck and call, and the country enjoyed the fruits of peacetime. For Adams, things were rougher almost from the start. He was a trailblazer on issues involving states' rights, political parties, and the threat of war with France. He didn't always handle these issues successfully, but even his failures were instructive.

The threat of war with France was a major headache throughout Adams's administration, and the U.S. and France secured peace just as Adams was leaving office. Throughout Adams's term, French vessels antagonized American trading ships on grounds of complicity with Britain. A major war would have been a logistical nightmare. The young

United States, barely independent, wished to avoid any war, especially one with a European superpower like France, which had a huge army and navy. Adams struggled to raise the funds to build a navy consisting of just two ships. The country's biggest cities—Boston, Philadelphia, and New York—lent ships to the federal government, but it was clear that if war came, French forces would dwarf those of the U.S.

Moreover, the idea of war with France was a sore spot for many Americans. They remembered that the French aided American troops during the American Revolution and they cheered when the French experienced their own revolution in 1789. France was like America's sibling in its pursuit of liberty and equality. To many Americans, especially the Republicans, declaring war against the revolutionary French regime was off-limits. Adams understood these sentimental ties to France. He had been an envoy to France after the American Revolution and was a personal friend of the freedom fighter Marquis de Lafayette. But Adams was also a defender of big business interests in America that depended on safe, free trade routes on the high seas. He was a harsh critic of the anarchy into which he feared France was sinking. As a result, Adams favored war in principle.

The **division of American policitians** into **two main parties spawned a** lively **new brand** of **mudslinging.**

The resulting tension between France and the U.S. took years to resolve, and the issue unfortunately made Adams appear wishy-washy and indecisive.

With the threat of war ever-present on the international front, Adams also had a big problem on the domestic front—the rise of party politics. Parties were a major source of anxiety for Adams, one that his predecessor never had to worry about. Washington was elected unanimously, so he never faced any serious political opponents who didn't like him or his policies. Adams had a far different experience. He felt opposition at every turn. His political adversaries began to join forces, grouping themselves into what eventually became the party of the Jeffersonian Republicans. On the other side were the Federalists, with whom Adams was allied. The Republicans had many complaints with Adams. They claimed he wanted to strong-arm the formation of a powerful federal government that would outrank state and local governments. They were outraged when he played fast and loose with citizens' rights by allowing the (admittedly draconian) Alien and Sedition Acts to become law.

This division of American politicians into two main parties that thrived on dramatic antagonism spawned a lively new brand of mudslinging in both congressional debate and popular journalism. Adams was a basically sensitive soul, unaccustomed to the harsh exaggerations of polemic. He often felt hurt when senators mocked his girth by calling him "His Rotundity" or implied that he was insane (as Alexander Hamilton did). In his letters to Abigail, Adams sometimes wrote of how these personal attacks depressed him. And his feelings are understandable, for he was arguably the primary guinea pig for that now storied American tradition of political mudslinging.

Adams responded to the Republicans' slings and arrows by trying to rise above the party system altogether. McCullough points out that this effort was misguided—basically an attempt to deny the reality of American politics. In fact, this mistake may well have cost Adams a second term in office. In 1799, he unexpectedly reversed his pro-war position toward France, appointing an American envoy to conclude a peace treaty with the French. The hawkish Federalists were aghast and felt betrayed. Even Adams's own secretary of state, Timothy Pickering, wrote that the president's sudden reversal of policy left "the *honor* of the country . . . prostrated in the dust." McCullough suggests that the Federalists' anger and sense of betrayal weakened the support that Adams desperately needed in the tight elections of 1800.

At the heart of Adams's difficult relations with both his own party and the Republicans were big questions. What did the presidency mean to the new nation? What *should* it mean? Adams was the first president to have to work this out. By nature he believed firmly in democracy and in the American government's balance of power system. Yet his enemies often accused him of being a closet monarchist or aristocrat who wanted the president to be a king. Adams's unfortunate insistence that the U.S. president should be addressed as "His Majesty" didn't exactly exonerate him of those charges. The conflict was real, and Adams was torn. He felt that the young nation needed a firm hand and a strong central leadership to guide it, but he also felt that Americans should be more fully entrusted with the task of self-government. The history of the United States in the two centuries after Adams shows that this basic conflict is still with us—but he was the first to face it squarely.

A CHANGING NATION

Another of Adams's major headaches was the growing gap between city and countryside during his time. Washington never worried about keeping the union together in spirit. But the new political schism between the Federalists and Republicans was also a geographical one. While Adams had the firm backing of New England, his support in the nation's outlying regions was less sure. Republican clout was centered in Virginia, which had no urban population. The party's appeal to the sizable and quickly growing number of rural Americans was considerable. As McCullough remarked in an interview with his publisher, we must remember that Adams and his son John Quincy Adams were for many decades the only American presidents not from Southern slave-holding states.

The weight of public opinion against a president from faraway New England was a serious obstacle. Country dwellers distrusted what they considered high-handed Federalist city officials, like Adams, who had a

"Washington was immensely popular, elected unanimously, and all but impervious to criticism. Adams had no loyal following as Washington had."

reputation for being too citified, too civilized, and too eager to import European high culture to the free shores of America. In 1799, rural anger at the federal government exploded when a farmer from southeastern Pennsylvania, John Fries, led a rebellion against unfair taxes. The rebellion was quickly squelched, but the question of what to do with Fries remained. Adams's advisers all counseled execution, which was prescribed by law. But after giving the matter further consideration, Adams ended up pardoning Fries on the official grounds that the insurrection had no calamitous consequences. But there was a deeper reason for the pardon. Adams rightly sensed that Fries had become a symbol of rural America. He hoped that a pardon would help heal the rift between the urban power centers and the frontier regions. But Adams's honorable pardon made the Federalists, who believed that the frontier rednecks needed to be kept on a tight leash, even more upset with him.

REMEMBERING ADAMS

Adams's career is studded with successes as well as with hardships. But like the figure of Adams himself, his successes were often behind the scenes and overshadowed by the flashier achievements of others. His courageous willingness to cross the Atlantic in the horrible winter of 1778 to strengthen relations between France and the newly independent U.S. paid off handsome dividends for America on the foreign relations scene. His tedious, months-long pursuit of Dutch loans was eventually successful, enabling the establishment of an American national bank that could mint its own currency and put the American economy on solid footing. Adams's wary approach to the prospect of war with France may have seemed cowardly to many pro-war Federalists at the time, but in hindsight we see that it saved America the unthinkable costs of war at a moment when the young nation couldn't afford them. Adams's insistence on a strong national defense left the country with a sizable naval fleet by the end of his term. In this way, Adams set the tone for later presidents who would advocate a healthy American military in the name of defense, not aggression.

In any case, Adams's record of achievements is not what makes him such a sympathetic character in McCullough's biography. Rather, it's the portrait of a beleaguered and overworked Adams, a fretful president personally wounded by journalistic slurs and opponents' attacks, that makes him so likable. In our own times, when attacks on the image and idea of America have led many Americans to question the nation's role in the world, the hardworking Adams is almost *more* appealing than other, more glamorous Founding Fathers. An ordinary working man trudging behind the scenes, Adams may be the real hero for our times.

The Supporting Players

Adams was a key figure among our nation's founders—but has been overshadowed by some of his more colorful counterparts.

○ ○ ○

JOHN ADAMS

As the first vice president and the second president of the newly formed United States, John Adams earned a glamorous and important role in American history. But in some ways, he was ill-suited for that role. In an era that produced political superstars, Adams was cut from more modest material. There's no doubt that he was competent and committed and that he performed his duties thoroughly and thoughtfully. He poured all his energy into his work. At the end of his life, he commented that no one should ever envy the president, so difficult is his job.

Adams knew few luxuries during his sturdy New England upbringing and was accustomed to doing his share without complaint. He put up with hardships that few others would have accepted. He willingly crossed the Atlantic in the frigate *Boston* during the terrible winter of 1778 to serve as an envoy to France. He spent long, lonely months in Amsterdam, separated from his wife and family, without even being received by the public officials he needed to meet. As president, he avoided war with France despite heavy criticism from both his own party and the opposition. He put his nose to the grindstone for his nation at a crucial time in its history, and his achievements were essential. Many of Adams's achievements, like his securing of much-needed Dutch loans for the young American economy, required modest perseverance rather than brilliant heroism. Regardless, these achievements are no less important.

Still, dedicated patriots and hard workers don't automatically become famous or beloved figures. In fact, Adams's industriousness may be the very reason why he's less recognized today than his contemporaries who had flashier personalities. Adams lacked the charisma and attractiveness of Thomas Jefferson, the cragginess and heroism of George Washington, and the cleverness and wily charms of Benjamin Franklin. Adams's physical appearance—less important then in a politician than now, but still significant—was comical rather than formidable, with his huge belly and bald head. As a quick thinker, Adams was no match for his son John Quincy. As a financial strategist, he was no match for Abigail, who urged him to get into government securities when they could have made a fortune. Adams prided himself on his intellect, but he admitted that he couldn't write very well. As McCullough notes, Adams's first published book is largely a smattering of quotations from other authors, who are not always cited. Adams's temper was

> Adams's **temper was** sometimes unmanageable, and many of his contemporaries called him unbalanced.

sometimes unmanageable, and many of his contemporaries called him unbalanced. One unsympathetic newspaper columnist claimed Adams was insane. Adams identified his own worst fault as his vanity, his excessive focus on himself and his reputation—a judgment that most of his opponents (and even some of his allies) shared.

Of course, the Founding Fathers each had their faults, so we can't unfairly single Adams out. But it's useful to remember Adams's faults as a way of appreciating his character and his particular role in American history. In a sense he was a trailblazer in *not* being glamorous. Despite the many accusations that he was an aristocrat, Adams's ordinariness makes him more similar to the average American than Jefferson or Washington could ever be. For Adams, holding public office wasn't a glory but a job—a difficult job that required a lot of drudgery and brought little happiness or peace of mind. Adams sought elected office not for privilege and honor but for the good he could do for his country. In today's media-dominated political culture, in which snazzy sound bites often matter more than hard work or devotion to ideals, Adams provides a healthy example of a politician who excelled at serving his nation simply by caring intensely and working hard.

THOMAS JEFFERSON

The fascinating Thomas Jefferson shines throughout *John Adams,* probably in part because McCullough originally intended the book to be a parallel biography of both Adams and Jefferson. Jefferson was Adams's friend, colleague, and rival. They both played important roles in the founding of America and they shared a lengthy and fascinating personal relationship. When the two were posted in Europe on diplomatic business for the young American republic, they spent an enormous amount of time in each other's company. Adams had his portrait painted with a book of Jefferson's in the background, and Jefferson always kept a bust of Adams near his desk at Monticello, Jefferson's home in Virginia.

Yet it's the contrast between Jefferson and Adams that catches our fancy, for they were very different men. In many ways, Jefferson had the more intriguing personality. While McCullough eventually decided to focus on Adams alone, Jefferson's colorful character sometimes makes us wish we heard less about Adams and more about Jefferson.

Jefferson certainly outdoes Adams in the vibrancy of his personal life. Adams was dumpy and bald. Jefferson was slim, tall, and strikingly handsome. Adams lived carefully and modestly, always aware of the consequences of each action. Jefferson lived his life freely on a big scale, doing exactly as he pleased, risking (and finding) scandal by allegedly becoming sexually involved with a black slave woman named Sally Hemings. Adams believed in New England frugality. Jefferson expanded his palatial Virginia compound without giving a second thought to his already huge debts. He was addicted to shopping, buying no fewer than sixty-two paintings during a single stay in Paris. Adams believed devoutly in law and order. Jefferson once shocked Abigail Adams by telling her that a little rebellion is good now and then.

These personal details about Jefferson are more than random trivia. They help define his whole belief system and show us the sharp political differences between him and Adams. Jefferson was a Romantic figure along the lines of the English poet Lord Byron. He was somewhat disdainful of social conventions and was committed to individual freedom. For Jefferson, the American Revolution was an opportunity to bring to life his Romantic vision of individual liberty and unlimited potential—a vision that's at the core of the American dream. More than the pleasure-seeking scientist Franklin or the ever-reliable Washington, Jefferson is a mythical figure in American history because he was so committed to this idealist dream. He was a true visionary.

Adams, by contrast, was no dreamer. Yes, he had lofty ideas about what was good for America, but his goals—a strong federal government and a powerful national defense—were more practical. But Adams's more concrete concerns weren't necessarily less important than Jefferson's big dreams. Practicality and idealism both play key roles in American culture. But without Jefferson, the American dream would be considerably less majestic than it is.

Jefferson's and Adams's different political visions led to some sharp disagreements. Jefferson strongly opposed war with the revolutionary French regime, which he saw as a noble emblem of rebellion against tyranny. The more hawkish Adams thought France posed a threat to American business interests and national security. Jefferson supported strong states' rights, which Adams feared could be a threat to national unity. Jefferson supported the Kentucky Resolutions, which gave state legislatures the "natural right" to reject federal actions they found to be unconstitutional—a stance that was a slap in the face to Adams. All in all, the individual disagreements between Jefferson and Adams added up to fundamentally incompatible belief systems. A rift between them was

A democrat to the core

Of all the Founding Fathers, Jefferson was perhaps the purest believer in the democratic ideal. During his presidential term, he instituted the thoroughly democratic custom of shaking hands rather than bowing at official White House receptions. Jefferson also wrote his own epitaph in true democratic fashion, mentioning his authorship of the Declaration of Independence and his founding of the University of Virginia but conspicuously omitting any mention that he was president of the United States.

unavoidable. In a foreword that Jefferson wrote for a political bestseller of the time, he made a sly reference to political "heresies" spreading throughout the nation—a remark everyone interpreted to be aimed at Adams. Readers saw Jefferson accusing Adams of moving away from the cause of freedom and returning to British authoritarian politics. Matters only worsened when Adams's son John Quincy defended his father in a series of anonymous articles. Eventually, the feud between Adams and Jefferson escalated, and the two men did not speak for many years.

Jefferson and Adams eventually revived their friendship, but Jefferson appears to have been less interested in it than Adams was. Perhaps Jefferson, who by that time had been president himself, simply didn't have enough time to reply to all of Adams's frequent letters. Adams jokingly complained that several of his own letters must be worth one of Jefferson's—but the self-deprecation rings a little less than genuine. Adams may have never entirely gotten over the rift with Jefferson, and his relationship with Jefferson may have been affected by Adams's envy of Jefferson's political clout and charisma. But despite their falling out, Adams and Jefferson both played crucial roles in the early days of America. The fact that Jefferson and Adams died on the same day—the national holiday of July 4, 1826—stands as a bizarrely fated conclusion of their collaboration and friendship.

ABIGAIL ADAMS

Abigail is a figure of great strength in McCullough's biography. Much more than her predecessor, Martha Washington, Abigail showed the young America that a strong first lady could be a great resource. She seems to have been as much of a confidante and adviser to Adams as she was a spouse and lover, even from the beginning. Later, one of Abigail's portraitists declared that she must have been a perfect Venus, the goddess of love and beauty, in her younger years. In reality, though, Adams's relationship with her was never fiery or steamy. "Dear friend" and "My dearest friend" are typical openers to their letters to each other. Adams's nickname for Abigail was Portia, in tribute to the Roman wife of Brutus, who represents noble self-sacrifice—not exactly an erotic pet name.

In an era when wives were typically consigned to domestic duties, Abigail's role as friend, counselor, and assistant to Adams was remarkable.

She was always hardheaded and practical. When Adams was posted in Paris, Abigail's requests for French luxury items never sprang from personal greed or whim. Instead, she traded silk gloves, ribbon, thread, and fans for household staples desperately needed back home. "Handkerchiefs will turn to good account for hard money," she wrote to Adams in one letter. Abigail's keen business sense led her to try to persuade her husband to invest in government securities rather than in real estate. When he refused, he lost an opportunity to make a fortune.

Yet Abigail's practicality did not make her hard-hearted or frigid. Her letters to Adams when he was away in Europe are rich with emotion, expressing tender yearnings to see him again. Amazingly, she does not resent his extended absence. Stuck in Braintree, Massachusetts, with young children to care for, her tone is strikingly patient and uncomplaining. Even during a mysterious period in which Adams virtually stopped writing her altogether, Abigail never whined, allowing herself only a few scattered comments about how she would appreciate more letters. To a great extent, Abigail's patience stemmed from her understanding of the stakes of Adams's diplomatic business. She knew that the fate of America was largely in her husband's hands. Her wisdom and understanding makes her a more sympathetic character than her husband when in dealing with emotional problems and family crises. She felt pity for her wayward, bankrupt son Charles when Adams announced that he would disown the young man.

In an era when wives were all too often consigned to domestic duties, Abigail's role in Adams's life was remarkable.

Abigail was also a shrewd politician. Observers of the Adams presidency often commented on how much of the job she performed behind the scenes. In fact, Abigail sometimes attracted a bit of the scorn that Hillary Clinton attracted almost two centuries later—criticism that the first lady was too much of a busybody in her husband's affairs and that she should leave the president's work to the president. Others more generously remarked that Abigail had more innate ability than Adams did, and they welcomed her sway over him. McCullough notes that Abigail's political wisdom would have come in handy when Adams disastrously recommended that President Washington be addressed as "His Majesty." Years earlier, on her first trip to Europe, Abigail had explained to a snooty Scotsman that Americans respected merit, not titles. If she had been around to give a few words of advice before his speech to the Senate, Adams might have rethought his position and realized that "His Majesty" would be unpopular in a new democratic nation. In short, listening to his wife might have spared him a lot of embarrassment.

Abigail was not a diva. She lacked the formidable power of Eleanor Roosevelt, the charm of Dolly Madison, and the glamour of Jackie Kennedy. She never seems to have attracted fans, whether in New York, Paris, or London. Abigail behaved appropriately but she never shone. At heart, she was an intelligent, publicity-shy, modest New England housewife who wandered into the national spotlight, but never let the attention go to her head. Like her husband, Abigail was sincerely moved by a desire for public service, for doing good work for her country and her husband.

BENJAMIN FRANKLIN

Franklin is one of the stars of early American history, and we naturally look forward to his cameo appearances in the pages of *John Adams*. But McCullough's portrait of Franklin may come as a surprise to those who received a very different introduction to him in school textbooks—and one of the reasons why *John Adams* is sometimes referred to as revisionist history. McCullough doesn't aim to discredit Franklin utterly. On the contrary, at times he shows us the traditional view of Franklin's success as a diplomat and a scientist who was also one of the wealthiest people in America and had a huge circle of fans both at home and abroad.

But when we read that few could understand a word Franklin said when he spoke French to his admirers in Paris, we see a different side. Franklin loved his Parisian lifestyle, which included sipping champagne at court functions like a native aristocrat and renting a palatial home that shocked Adams with its price tag. This Franklin is a far cry from the frugal man who taught us "A penny saved is a penny earned" in *Poor Richard's Almanack*, his early book of American wisdom. It's also surprising to learn that the author of the aphorism "Early to bed, early to rise, makes a man healthy, wealthy, and wise" actually got up very late in the morning. Franklin also fathered an illegitimate son, who became quite successful. And we discover that the man known for his devotion to the new American nation actually had little to contribute when attending official meetings. In fact, Franklin's silence puzzled Adams, who saw it bordering on indifference.

But McCullough by no means makes fun of Franklin. Franklin's luxurious French lifestyle wasn't necessarily a disadvantage: to act like a Parisian when in Paris, especially while on a delicate diplomatic mission, was probably wise. As envoys, Franklin and Adams were trusted with securing French recognition and trade for the newly formed United States—an urgent and important job. In terms of recognizing and accepting local customs, Franklin was likely a far more effective diplomat than Adams. In fact, Adams spent his first few months in France expressing revulsion at local morals and tastes in clothing. Franklin found Adams's insensitivity irritating, believing it could threaten the success of their diplomatic mission. In Franklin's view, Adams was too obstinate: Adams refused to thank the French sufficiently for their support of America and claimed that it was America that deserved French gratitude. Franklin thought Adams was too high and mighty, and he wrote a letter to Congress saying so: "I apprehend that he mistakes his ground." Franklin's letter implies that he saw it as a significant part of his job to correct Adams's errors.

On the whole, it's hard to fault Franklin for his opinion of Adams. He was a more experienced diplomat than Adams—and a more successful one, considering his success in drumming up general French enthusiasm

Basking in the limelight

Franklin was apparently no master of the French language, but that didn't keep him from taking France by storm. The level of celebrity and recognition Franklin attained during his French diplomatic stints was truly without parallel—and he loved it. Adams, who witnessed the Franklin-in-France phenomenon firsthand, later wrote, "[Franklin's] name was familiar to government and people . . . to such a degree that there was scarcely a peasant or a citizen, a *valet de chambre,* coachman or footman, a lady's chambermaid or a scullion in a kitchen, who was not familiar with it, and who did not consider him as a friend to human kind."

for things American. Adams's New England bluntness may have worked well in Boston and New York City, but it may have been a disadvantage in the more genteel Paris. Seeing Adams through Franklin's critical eyes helps us understand the second president from a different angle. Adams's no-nonsense mindset may have threatened his political success in some areas at least as much as it advanced it in others.

GEORGE WASHINGTON

Washington is the best known and probably the best loved figure of early American history. His commanding presence and star status posed a challenge for someone working in his shadow and a significant obstacle for his successor. Washington enjoyed virtually universal devotion and acclaim and was elected unanimously. He was a talented general and a natural leader with an innate dignity of character and poise in public. Adams, though talented in his own ways, displayed none of these overtly awe-inspiring gifts. Interestingly, it was Adams himself who called upon the Continental Congress to name Washington commander-in-chief of the army.

As vice president under this great leader, Adams made only a few stumbles. The tensions that arose between Washington and Adams tell us much about the challenge they faced in building a new democratic government. One issue that came between the two men was Adams's embarrassing insistence on a fancy title like "His Majesty" for the American president—an idea almost no one in Congress supported. It proved to be a particularly sore spot for Washington, since his native Virginians came to hate Adams's position on this issue. They feared it revealed a dangerous and antidemocratic affinity for the aristocracy on Adams's part. When Washington heard that Adams had become "odious" in Virginia, he began to distance himself from his vice president. In an interesting twist, McCullough speculates that Washington's distance from Adams helped define the role of the vice president at this early stage of American politics, diminishing forever what could have been a more vital role.

Personal wealth was another issue that came between Washington and Adams. Like Benjamin Franklin, Washington was one of the richest men in America, holding vast tracts of land in Virginia and the Midwest. Adams, on the other hand, often had to struggle to make ends meet—he

sent handkerchiefs back from Paris for Abigail to trade for household staples when times were particularly tough. We might suppose that public
officials' personal finances wouldn't matter much in the long run, but it's
naïve to believe so. In early America, income level frequently dictated
assumptions and beliefs. The wealthy Washington and Franklin, for example, believed that government officials—including the president—should
serve without pay. They maintained that such a volunteer position would
be immune to corruption, since only men with high-minded motives of
public service would ever be interested in holding it. They believed that
such a system would ensure that lowly thoughts of money and profit would
never dirty the high office.

The less wealthy Adams thought otherwise. In his view, if the presidency were an unpaid position, it would be monopolized by the only
class of Americans able to work for free—the wealthy. Adams feared that
the rich and elite would take over the government, while the more "middling ranks," as he called the middle class, would have no representation.
As McCullough wryly notes, those middling ranks included Adams himself. He certainly had a personal stake in the question of pay for public
officials, since as vice president he was about to set up a household in the
expensive capital city of New York.

The issue also sheds light on how thoroughly Adams's practical New
England background influenced his policy decisions. Adams didn't share
the idealistic dreams of democracy that only the extremely rich like Washington could afford to entertain. Adams understood that a government
post was a job like any other. It wasn't a mere honorary position but one
that demanded real labor and occasional hardship. A salary was a way of
recognizing this fact. Maybe most important, a salary placed the president
on more or less the same footing as other working Americans. In this light,
it's ironic that so many of Adams's contemporaries derided him as a
wanna-be aristocrat who was out of touch with the common man. In fact,
Adams's position on government salaries was meant as a subtle message to
the population—a government official wasn't a larger-than-life figure
buoyed by enormous wealth, but just a man trying to do his job like everyone else. Despite Washington's extraordinary and unsurpassed popularity,
he probably could never have understood the importance of this connection between the president and the people.

JOHN QUINCY ADAMS

John Quincy Adams grew up in an atmosphere of public service and politics. He was a true insider. At the tender age of fourteen, he accompanied his father on a diplomatic mission to the court of France, learning about cultural differences and international codes of etiquette in a way that few teenagers could. A few years later, he was sent on a solo trip to the court of Catherine the Great in St. Petersburg, becoming one of the first Americans to visit Russia.

But John Quincy was no spoiled son of power. He didn't sit back and enjoy the privileges of his father's power and prestige like his younger brother Charles, who had the same background but ended up bankrupt. John Quincy was intellectually gifted, seemingly more so than his father. But more important, he worked with amazing industriousness to develop his talents. He excelled at Harvard. When he turned to the study of French on his trip to Paris with his father, he quickly surpassed the elder Adams's facility with the language. John Quincy was known for his elegant way with words and his talent for lucid explanations. During the acrimonious Publicola affair, in which Thomas Jefferson and an anonymous critic carried out a bitter policy debate in public, many suspected that "Publicola" was John Adams. But James Madison maintained that Publicola was the young John Quincy, whose writing was notably more eloquent than his father's. The son's intellectual superiority to his father in certain respects was common knowledge at the time.

John Quincy's public role and his father's involvement in it helped define popular views on political power in America. The question of an inherited presidency was one of the sore spots of John Quincy Adams's career—something his innate intelligence and leadership skills could never entirely dispel. To many people in early nineteenth-century America, John Quincy's rise to power came dangerously close to a European-style passing of titles from father to son. People worried that such a dynasty could undermine democracy. The elder Adams was suspected of being partial to aristocracy ever since his lengthy stay at the courts of Europe and his plea to Congress to bestow an honorific title on the presidency. When John Quincy showed interest in becoming president much later, those popular suspicions came back with a vengeance. The elder Adams didn't help matters, since he did use a lot of clout to help his son get elected in the 1824 elections, which were nearly a stalemate. John Adams called on Speaker of the House Henry Clay to help break the tie when the vote passed to the House of Representatives.

On the whole, though, it's hard to judge this father-son solidarity too harshly. John Adams's joy at his son's success is heartwarming. When the elder Adams learned that John Quincy had won every single vote in Quincy, Braintree, and Weymouth, Massachusetts, he called it one of the most gratifying events of his life. It's difficult to begrudge an eighty-nine-year-old his fatherly pride. Indeed, John Quincy's later career was a fine one. Yet the fact remains that the father's role in his son's electoral success does smack a bit of nepotism, at least to many modern-day observers—and to many of John Quincy's contemporaries too. The prospect of a son inheriting the presidency didn't arise again for a long time. The multiple presidencies of the Adams family may have raised American concerns over monarchy and undue influence in voting, making voters all the more determined to base their presidential choices on individual character and achievement.

A President But No Politician

Adams's unglamorous, no-nonsense style would likely have made him an ugly duckling in the media circus of today's politics.

○   ○   ○

How do you think John Adams would have fared as president in the twenty-first century?

THE IMAGE PROBLEM

Before wondering how well Adams would do in office today, we need to ask whether he could win an election in the first place. It's indisputable that the race for president today is much more of a media game than it was in the 1790s (though the media played a significant role even then). So we have to consider Adams's public persona, his charisma, and his ability to sway voters with the right image and the right talk. Many of Adams's acquaintances described him as a man of passion, but it's not clear that it came across in Adams's public speaking. Observers of his Senate addresses agree that he was clear and persuasive but not very dynamic. In that light, it's doubtful he could have whipped up applause before a television audience.

Another important factor is Adams's physical appearance—a consideration that 1790s politicians would have considered trivial but that is undeniably important today. Adams wasn't exactly an overwhelming physical presence. His shape—short, fat, and bald—and his penchant for impressive titles earned him the derisive nickname "His Rotundity." It's hard to imagine anyone publicly called such a name being successful in televised debates. The tall, slim, and elegantly handsome Jefferson would have done far better. Modern American history offers the example of Richard Nixon and John F. Kennedy. Nixon may have been brighter and more knowledgeable than Kennedy in their famous 1960 debate, but Nixon's poor TV presence—hunched stature, uneasy physical manner, dark facial stubble—essentially lost him the debate. Unfair though it may be, the presidency of our time is an image and popularity contest, and Adams likely wouldn't have had what it takes to win it.

Unfair though it may be, the presidency of our time is an image and popularity contest, and Adams likely wouldn't have had what it takes to win it.

But Adams's strong pro-business stance would likely have helped him today. The "half-war" he waged with revolutionary France for years showed his readiness to use the military to defend American interests, especially economic and business interests. One of the goals of those who favorewd war with France was to guarantee the right of American ships to trade with European ports without the threat of French attack. Then, as now, the aims of big business played a significant role in a presi-dent's popularity. Anything that promised business expansion would've benefited Adams's political standing. True, Americans considered France a friend of the American Revolution and a brother in the fight against tyr-anny. But even so, Adams sensed that practical affairs like free trade were more important to the population than sentimental ideals about freedom fighting. In this regard, Adams differed sharply from Jefferson, who strongly objected to war with France and held an idealistic admiration for the French Revolution—a love based on noble philosophical principles, not on concerns for business and trade. Jefferson may have done well in the idealistic 1960s or 1970s, but in the 2000s, a hard-nosed respect for business interests seems to be more effective for winning elections.

On the other hand, there's no guarantee that Adams's warmongering would bring him support today. He might abandon his hawkish mindset just as he did in 1798, when he suddenly and unexpectedly appointed an

American minister to the French government, effectively ending war preparations. Adams's own Federalist Party members were outraged. One of them even announced he hoped that Adams's horses might break Adams's neck on his way back to Boston. We might imagine a similar scenario today if a Republican president heavily in favor of war with a country suddenly retreated and became a pacifist. Such a leader would likely be labeled wishy-washy and lose favor even among his own party. He might be able to salvage his reputation by supporting military spending in the name of defense, as Adams did when he committed large funds to expand and refurbish the U.S. Navy. The navy's fleet of fifty ships by 1800 was owed in large part to Adams's unfailing support for a strong national defense. Perhaps large-scale military spending would heighten Adams's popularity if he were president today, as it heightened Ronald Reagan's popularity in the 1980s.

On top of Adams's personal appearance and policy stance is the question of his overall image. Today, Adams might have trouble securing a broad base of support simply for geographic and cultural reasons. Now, even more so than in the 1790s, America is a vast country steeped with a pioneer spirit. Many Americans today like their leaders to be seemingly adventurous, outdoors friendly, big-spirited, and not overly citified. George H.W. Bush ditched his civilized East Coast origins to set up camp in the frontier-spirit state of Texas. Bill Clinton played up his down-home rural Arkansas roots over his background as a Rhodes scholar and Yale Law graduate.

In this regard, Adams's upbringing might have been detrimental to him today. He was used to a simple and well-ordered New England life. He was frugal and cautious, afraid of debt more than almost anything else. Today, American life is anything but simple and well-ordered. The U.S. economy thrives on the debt industry, making a deeply indebted shopping addict like Jefferson a better spokesman for contemporary America than the penny-pinching Adams. Also, Jefferson hailed from Virginia, a state virtually without urban areas. He understood the political mindset of a mostly rural population. Of course, Adams at times showed a similar understanding of the backwoods population. In matters of policy he actually was more committed to rural America than he might appear, as was the case in his high-minded pardon of the rebel John Fries, a Pennsylvania farmer. In rejecting the advice of his cabinet by pardoning Fries, Adams showed not only mercy for this particular man but also sensitivity to the plight of the average farmer. The question is whether this common-man sensibility would have helped Adams today. As we see today, political success is built not on actions alone, but on spin. Adams in the twenty-first century would have to overhaul his buttoned-down, civilized image.

○ ○ ○

The hot-and-cold friendship between Adams and Jefferson was lengthy and tumultuous. What issues came between these two men?

LIKE OIL AND WATER

Adams and Jefferson had very different social and cultural backgrounds. Fate threw them together in the founding of their nation's government. Their friendly relations were a result of this collaboration—otherwise, in different times or a different country, we might doubt that the two would've given each other the time of day. Yes, both were well read, literate, and educated in the classics. And both cared devoutly about the future of their new nation. But in their broader outlooks on life they had almost nothing in common.

Jefferson was a lover of luxury. He wore the clothes of a dandy, built a palatial mansion, and sent back to America no fewer than sixty-two paintings he purchased on a single trip to Paris. Adams was a plain-living gentleman farmer, brought up in a simple wooden frame house and accustomed to a life of New England thriftiness. He shied away from all forms of conspicuous consumption unless his career dictated it. Jefferson lived in constant debt, owing thousands of dollars to British and Dutch bankers throughout his career. Adams abhorred the very thought of debt—he would never even take a personal loan. Jefferson was in the mold of a Romantic hero: galloping for hours through the woods after the tragic death of his wife, cherishing an idealized love for freedom and beauty and living a secluded life of contemplation in the countryside.

Adams was much more of a pragmatist who valued a nose-to-the-grind-stone work ethic above all else. Given these differences, what's surprising isn't that Jefferson and Adams suffered a rift in their friendship in later years, but that they ever managed to be friends at all.

Yet the two were friends for a long while. Their friendship is much more than a private detail in the lives of two Founding Fathers: it stands as a symbol of national diversity, of the power of a common cause to bring together Americans from vastly different walks of life. Adams and Jefferson spent several years in each other's regular company in Paris during the long struggle for loans and American diplomatic representation abroad. Abigail Adams wrote that Jefferson "add[ed] much to the social circle" when he was present. After the Adamses moved to London, Abigail and Jefferson traded shopping lists for their different cities. Jefferson missed the Adams's company, writing to them that he was "in the dumps" after their departure. There was clearly a casual and friendly intimacy among the two men and their families. But the connection was based on shared ideas and beliefs as well as on socializing. When Adams was sitting for a portrait in 1785, he chose to be portrayed with Jefferson's *Notes on the State of Virginia* clearly displayed at his side—an emblem of his esteem for his friend.

But in the more difficult political times of the 1790s, Adams and Jefferson's friendship fell apart. Things grew especially tense as America grew fearful of war with France and politicians divided into opposing camps. Of course, part of the tension arose from the fact that the two friends ran against each other in the presidential election. The electoral system at the time made things even more awkward because the runner-up automatically became vice president. Becoming Adams's political subordinate was difficult for the proud Jefferson—especially since he lost to Adams by only three electoral votes.

Serious political differences also began to divide the two men. During Adams's tenure as president, the two main political camps that had always existed in America started to crystallize into the two-party structure we know today—the Federalists and the Republicans. Adams was wary of identifying too strongly with either of these emerging parties, but his beliefs and policies were solidly on the Federalist side. The Federalists stressed the need for a strong central government, believing that handing too much authority to state governments was dangerous. Their motto in matters of government was "law and order." The Republicans, whose ranks included Jefferson and many other Southerners, saw the government as the voice of the people rather than a giant policeman looming over them. We might distill the Republicans' motto as "freedom for all."

These party differences came to a head in the major U.S. foreign policy crisis of the 1790s—the question of how to handle revolutionary France. The French had long been friends of revolutionary America. They provided military supplies and manpower during the critical stages of the American Revolution. The French and American revolutionary causes also seemed similar. French freedom fighters claimed to be struggling for independence from the tyranny, unjust taxation, and social oppression of the aristocracy—the same reasons the Americans struggled against the British. In terms of ideals, the French and American revolutions both represented the noble fight for freedom.

> Where **Jefferson** stressed the **natural reason** of mankind, **Adams countered** that **humans** were **irrational** and **susceptible** to low **passions.**

This ideal was the aspect of the French Revolution that Jefferson loved. He was an ardent supporter of the French revolutionary cause, and he praised it in an article he published in the *Gazette of the United States* in 1790. He gushed about the cause of French freedom and how it represented "the blessings of self-government so long denied to mankind." If left alone, mankind would take care of itself just fine. The resulting self-government would be a blessing for all because people have a natural desire to do the sensible thing: "the sufficiency of human reason for the care of human affairs." Jefferson believed a Big Brother state was unnecessary and undesirable, for the will of the majority was "the only sure guardian of the rights of man."

Jefferson and his fellow Republicans mostly hailed from rural areas where there was no central power base. They preferred to see government as the spokesman for the entire scattered population, a way to allow the people to speak in one voice. So for Republicans like Jefferson, the French Revolution's war cries of equality and fraternity struck a chord. They saw France in the process of evolving a true popular voice, and they approved.

But the French Revolution disturbed Adams and other Federalists. For them, it wasn't a people's noble fight for freedom but the breakdown of order and security in a once-powerful state. Adams had always been concerned about safeguarding law and order in America, and he was horrified by what he saw as France's rapid slide into anarchy. Whereas Jefferson was enamored with the French ideals of a perfect society, Adams thought they were pipe dreams.

Adams wrote his own set of anonymous (but easily identifiable) series of articles in the *Gazette of the United States*. Whereas Jefferson praised the French Revolution, Adams emphasized that the human race would always be imperfect. "[T]he perfectibility of man is only human. . . . disease and vice will continue to disorder, and death to terrify mankind." Adams believed that the French got carried away and failed to recognize human shortcomings and the need for strong guidance from a powerful central government. Where Jefferson stressed the natural reason of mankind, Adams countered that humans were irrational and susceptible to low passions. Clearly, this debate involved more than France. Indirectly, the Federalists and Republicans were disagreeing about the role of government in America. Debate over the proper roles of Congress and the president never really came up during Washington's administration. But by 1790, these issues proved to be a major dividing point between Jefferson and Adams.

There were other rifts between Jefferson and Adams as well. One early crisis in the relationship began because of a set of hostile comments and misunderstandings between the two that appeared in print in 1791. Jefferson had warmly endorsed Thomas Paine's recently published *The Rights of Man*, a Republican rebuttal of the Federalists' (and British Tories') condemnation of the French Revolution. The endorsement appeared prominently on the title page of Paine's book. In it, Jefferson praised *The Rights of Man* as an antidote to some of the "political heresies" that were spreading throughout the nation. Though Jefferson later claimed he was shocked that the publisher used his endorsement in this way, the damage had already been done. It looked as if Jefferson was criticizing Adams and his policies. Indeed, Jefferson had told Washington privately that he had Adams in mind when he was writing about heresy.

In response to Jefferson's words, a series of articles, signed by an author calling himself "Publicola," began to appear in a Boston newspaper. Publicola attacked the idea that Adams's policies were heresy and asked whether Paine's book should be considered Holy Scripture. Most people assumed that Publicola was Adams himself, so the public thought a serious quarrel was brewing between Jefferson and Adams. In fact, Publicola was Adams's son John Quincy. Jefferson finally wrote a letter of apology to Adams, but the apology was rather stiff. Jefferson denied that he had ever had Adams in mind when referring to political heresies, despite having told Washington precisely the opposite. In effect, Jefferson apologized without taking responsibility for what had happened. Adams was understandably soured by the whole affair, and the two men stopped writing to each other for several years.

The relationship became even more awkward when the two men shared the reins of government starting in 1797. Adams won the highest number of electoral votes in the presidential elections, and Jefferson won the second highest. Under the electoral system at the time, the results meant that they became president and vice president, respectively. The political differences between them were compounded by their troubled personal relationship in the past. In short, they were unfortunate bedfellows whose political and personal disagreements were put center stage.

Soon, an issue arose that both Adams and Jefferson later remembered as a breaking point for their already shaky partnership—the question of which man should become envoy to revolutionary France after Adams's inauguration in 1797. Both men's original choice was James Madison, but then Adams changed his mind. For Jefferson, this was a clear signal that Adams was unduly influenced by the Federalists, who objected to the choice of Madison. This was repulsive to the freethinking Jefferson. According to a statement Jefferson made later, his conversation with Adams about the matter was the last time the two men ever talked about official government business—startling, considering it was just the beginning of Jefferson's term as vice president. The historical record seems to back up Jefferson's claim. The once-heavy correspondence between Jefferson and Adams dries up around this time. Adams was aware that he could never count on Jefferson in the way that Washington had once counted on Adams, now that party politics had come between them. The sacred trust seemed broken.

Yet the rift between the two men never became destructive. Remarkably, their strained relationship never threatened the presidency during Adams's term. It was a quiet and polite breakup, not an open war. Later in life, Adams and Jefferson began to correspond again, though never quite with their earlier enthusiasm. Adams was hurt that Jefferson never mentioned, much less offered condolences for, the death of Adams's son Charles. When Jefferson became president, Adams would complain half-jokingly that he only received one letter in reply to every four letters he wrote to Jefferson. The old camaraderie between the two was never completely extinguished, and the endurance of their friendship is as important as their falling out. While the waning of the Adams-Jefferson friendship may stand as a symbol of the rise of party politics in American government, the fact that the relationship never fully died out is also a symbol of the endurance of goodwill. Despite their differences, the warring factions within the early American government still managed to hang on to each other and preserve unity even in dissent.

○   ○   ○

What was Adams's character like? How did it figure into his political career?

AVOIDING THE SCANDAL SHEETS

By seemingly all accounts, Adams had a thoroughly upstanding character—a trait that makes him a rather bland figure for those who prefer sizzling history. His presidency was free of personal scandal, unlike his successor, Jefferson, whose reputed involvement with the slave woman Sally Hemings became the talk of the nation. Adams, though admittedly concerned with his own reputation, was seemingly untouched by greed and the lust for power. He never showed much interest in financial speculation or winning huge fortunes. Even when Abigail urged him to put money into lucrative national bonds, Adams was reluctant, preferring his more stable land investments. He was never swept away by mad passions. His relationship with Abigail endured years of separation, war, and political hardships, and her letters virtually always address him as "my dearest friend." There was one mysterious period when Adams's letter writing to Abigail slowed almost to a standstill while he was in Europe, but this is hardly evidence of marital discord. On the whole, Adams's family life was stable, and his role as father unimpeachable. There were difficulties—his daughter Nabby married a bankrupt rogue, and his son Charles became an alcoholic adulterer who also went bankrupt. True, Adams declared his intention to renounce Charles, which suggests a strain of cold-heartedness. But we do not know how serious Adams's threat was, since Charles died before Adams took any action. On the whole, throughout the ups and downs of American history during his lifetime and despite the personal disappointments and slights he suffered in his career, Adams was remarkably forbearing.

Jefferson called Adams "vain, irritable, and a bad calculator of the . . . motives which govern men."

But Adams himself was the first to admit his character flaws. While still a young man, he noted that vanity was his worst vice—not vanity in the sense of an obsession with his appearance but rather an inflated idea of his own importance in the world. Strikingly, Jefferson used the same word years later in discussing Adams's chief faults. Writing to his friend James Madison in 1786, Jefferson mentioned that Adams suffered from "a degree of vanity and blindness to it." After getting to know Adams more intimately by working with him in London for several weeks, Jefferson affirmed that his original verdict still stood. He called Adams "vain, irritable, and a bad calculator of the force and probably effect of the motives which govern men." Jefferson hastened to add that he loved Adams, but the vanity charge still stood.

Assuming we can trust Jefferson as a judge of character, his references to Adams's vanity suggest that Adams did have a problem with excessive self-regard. Of course, any presidential hopeful is perhaps bound to be a bit vain. But it's true that, at times, Adams seems to have been working at least as much for his own reputation as for the good of his country.

McCullough discusses Adams's deep desire for appreciation and recognition during Adams's diplomatic missions in Europe. When Adams returned from one of his overseas missions, he was bitterly disappointed that Congress failed to express gratitude for his effort. He felt as if he had been forgotten in Europe. On the whole, Adams indeed may have been a bit too preoccupied with how posterity would glorify his name.

Adams's vanity surely shaped his views. It must have inflated his idea of what the president or any public official should be. Adams's somewhat pompous side comes across in his preoccupation with the term of address for President Washington. He turned this issue into a major item for Congress to debate. Eager to do all he could to heighten the dignity of the federal government, Adams argued before the Senate that Washington deserved a more regal title than a mere "sir." He proposed "His Majesty the President." But in this regard Adams was out of step with the feelings of his countrymen, who were understandably skeptical of fancy titles that smacked of monarchy and aristocracy. One senator drew attention to the constitutional ban on titles. Yet Adams insisted on a more regal title, even to the point of making a fool of himself. To the amusement of many, someone even bestowed Adams with his own title — "His Rotundity."

In all the furor over Adams's insistence on fancy titles, it's impossible to forget that he viewed himself as "heir apparent" — the aristocratic term he himself used — to the presidency. If senators got used to calling Washington "His Majesty," then they would surely continue to call Adams the same when it was his turn. Mercy Warren, a former friend of the Adamses, later wrote that Adams's time among European aristocrats had corrupted him, that Adams was "beclouded by a partiality for monarchy." Of course, this statement is only speculation, but it's clear that suspicions of glory-seeking and vanity hounded Adams to the end.

In addition to his vanity, Adams also comes across as anxious and unschooled on human nature. He confessed to feeling great anxiety before almost every major decision. Jefferson, as we have seen, wrote that Adams was a "bad calculator" of the "motives which govern men." Others said similar things about Adams over the course of his life. Adams's misplaced trust in Alexander Hamilton is a good example. Hamilton maintained a façade of complete courtesy toward Adams but secretly worked against Adams almost from the beginning of their relationship. It was

Hamilton who privately urged several key politicians to put their support behind Washington during the first presidential elections. Adams was deeply disappointed over his poor share of the votes in those elections, but he seems never to have suspected Hamilton of meddling. Adams knew Hamilton was ambitious but thought the ambition was high-minded. This naïve faith in Hamilton became more damaging in 1798, when two members of Adams's cabinet took secret instructions from Hamilton—who was supposedly retired—about instigating war with France. It wasn't until much later that Adams began to suspect Hamilton of harboring desires to become the Napoleon of America. Had Adams been a little more perceptive about Hamilton earlier, he could have spared himself a lot of worry.

On the whole, there's nothing extreme about any of Adams's short-comings. Compared to many other American presidents, Adams was an angel. He guided the country through rough times and showed a heroic steadfastness, a commitment to his work, and a faith in America. His flaws aren't tragic moral vices. Rather, they're better characterized as limitations, obstacles that kept him from attaining higher stature. A crucial and tumultuous period like the 1790s required old-fashioned wisdom in its statesmen—an attribute Adams may have somewhat lacked. His vanity may have prevented him from becoming more successful. It may even have pushed him away from democracy and toward a fascination with grandeur, aristocrats, and monarchy. These limitations may explain why Adams never became a mythical figure like Washington, Franklin, and Jefferson did.

Adams has something of a reputation for cracking down on civil liberties and individual rights. Is this a fair judgment?

TIMES HAVE CHANGED

It's hard to look at Adams's civil rights record through a modern-day lens because he governed America during rather stormy times, when the nation was in a state of near-war with France. While there was never actually a formal declaration of war between France and the U.S., the American population and government took the prospect of war very seriously. Adams himself privately referred to the brewing conflict as the "half-war." The entire country was in a state of preparation. McCullough notes that Abigail Adams described Philadelphia at the time as a vast "military school" in training. New York, Boston, Philadelphia, and Baltimore all volunteered to lend locally built warships to the federal government to fend off any French naval attack. As the normally friendly French were suddenly characterized as enemies of the U.S., ordinary Americans and high officials alike became wary of foreigners in general.

This general climate of alarm in 1798 prompted the Alien and Sedition Acts—probably the most infamous products of Adams's administration. The Alien Act gave the president the right to deport any foreigner considered "dangerous," to use the blunt word of the original act. The most feared foreigners at the time were the estimated 25,000 French in the U.S., but other immigrant groups, such as the Irish, also drew suspicion—a hypocritical stance, considering that the vast majority of Americans at the time were the descendants of immigrants. Equally worrisome was the Sedition Act, which gave the government the right to fine or imprison anyone making "false, scandalous, and malicious" statements about the administration, Congress, or the president.

To be fair, we should first recall that Adams himself did not specifically request these acts. Congress, alarmed by fears of war, passed them into law without any provocation from the president. But as McCullough reminds us, Adams didn't veto the acts either, and his signature on them stands as one of the darkest mementoes of his presidency.

We may condemn Adams's actions, but we should remember how Americans have favored similar actions against foreigners during other times of war or near-war. The forced internment of Japanese-Americans during World War II and concerns about the possible deportation of innocent Arab-Americans in the wake of the attacks of September 11, 2001, remind us that Americans may all too quickly curtail civil liberties from those they don't consider American. The Alien Act may be unjust—even scandalously so—but it's certainly not unique in the history of the United States.

The Sedition Act is a different story. It was a blatant affront to the cherished principle of free speech guaranteed under the First Amendment. Even worse, whereas the Alien act was never invoked in any drastic way, the Sedition Act was applied frequently. Government officials tended to blur the dividing line between seditious statements and political criticism, using the Sedition Act as a way to censor Republicans who had been tormenting Adams for years. Indeed, McCullough notes that almost all those who were targeted under the Sedition Act were editors of Republican newspapers or journals—aside from occasional exceptions, like a tavern-goer in Hartford, Connecticut, who was taken into custody for criticizing the president a bit too harshly over a drink.

Adams's signature on the Alien and Sedition Acts stands as one of the darkest mementoes of his presdency.

In fairness, though, we should note that Adams's tacit support of the Sedition Act was far from unique among his fellow politicians. Many highly respected senators had wholly endorsed the bill. The renowned lexicographer Noah Webster announced that it was time to stop newspaper editors from slandering anyone they wished. Even the venerable George Washington commented in private that certain newspapers sorely deserved some punishment for their slanderous portrayals of American leaders. Among many American statesmen of the day, only Jefferson and a handful of others were against the Sedition Act. Allowing the measure to pass may have been an unconstitutional act, but Adams was by no means a tyrant imposing an unfair law on a whim.

Indeed, on other fronts, Adams's record displays a great respect for individual liberty. We see this tendency in Adams in his unexpected pardon of John Fries, a German-speaking farmer from Pennsylvania who briefly led other farmers in an armed revolt against federal tax collectors. The rebellion came to nothing, but Adams called in federal troops to maintain order. Fries was taken into federal custody, found guilty of treason, and condemned to die by hanging. He and his two henchmen appealed to Adams for a pardon. Somewhat surprisingly, Adams didn't reject the appeal out of hand, as his cabinet unanimously recommended, but instead sat down and reviewed the case thoroughly. McCullough notes that Adams's reluctance to carry out the execution was not due to any moral qualms about the death penalty itself. In fact, Adams strongly supported capital punishment in cases of treason and military desertion. Adams was cautious in the Fries case because he knew that important issues concerning rural America were at stake. Examining the motivations behind the Pennsylvania rebellion would be "a severe trial to my heart," Adams wrote, showing his personal commitment to justice for Fries and his heartfelt desire to understand rural America, both its good and its bad sides. Adams's conclusion was startling: Fries should be pardoned, since the insurrection didn't become a full-fledged rebellion. Adams's decision ignored the verdict of the jury handling the case and demonstrates his capacity for independent, conscientious action.

The Fries case is only one of many reasons to suspect that Adams's reputation for being hostile to individual liberties is exaggerated. In part, this reputation sprang from the later animosity between Adams and Jefferson. Their extended quarrel may have led both men to overemphasize the differences between their political stances—which in turn, may have led later historians to overemphasize these differences as well. In short, it's irresponsible to assert that Adams was a hard-nosed fascist while Jefferson cherished personal rights. By nature, Adams revered those rights deeply. He was not a snooty aristocrat content to trample on others' freedoms. His early activity in the legal circuits of rural New England left him with an indelible respect for the rights of the poor as well as the rich. If Adams had a fault in his attitude toward civil liberties, it was his excessive fear of the threat of political and social anarchy in wartime and his willingness to clamp down on individual rights in the name of national security.

Perhaps Adams's staunch support of civil liberties simply was outweighed by his belief that it was his duty to maintain order in the young nation by keeping a firm hand on freedom. A state of war can be a distressing time, and it's difficult to judge Adams too severely without keeping this in mind. After all, more than a few leaders in modern world history have used the "national emergency" decree as a carte blanche to rewrite their nations' laws as they please. Adams was no such despot. But his civil liberties record isn't entirely unimpeachable either.

○ ○ ○

Why did Adams lose his bid for a second term?

LEARNING POLITICAL LESSONS THE HARD WAY

To start, Adams didn't lose by much. The 1800 presidential election was extremely close. The rural voters' favorite, Thomas Jefferson, won 73 electoral votes across all sixteen states, as did the sly campaigner Aaron Burr. This tie resulted in a stalemate that took Congress months to resolve. The southerner Charles Pinckney got 64 electoral votes, with Adams barely ahead of Pinckney with 65. Because electoral votes are weighted differently, a small difference in any of a number of key voting districts could have made a substantial difference in the final electoral count. McCullough notes that with a mere 250 additional votes in New York City, Adams would have won. McCullough points out that it's ironic that Jefferson, a hater of cities, beat Adams in a city where Adams himself once held public office. Another complicating factor was the awkward system of including three-fifths of the slave population in electoral vote calculations. Slaves could not vote of course, but their numbers gave their masters' votes greater weight. Adams did not carry the South, where most American slaves resided, so this system worked against him.

Also, certain people stood in Adams's way. The sneaky Aaron Burr was one reason Adams failed to take the crucial New York City vote. Burr not only took votes away from Adams but also introduced a new style of heavy campaigning for which the old-fashioned Adams was unprepared. Even more important was Adams's ex-cabinet secretary Alexander Hamilton. In an inexplicable fit of propaganda that still puzzles historians today, Hamilton published a lengthy pamphlet lambasting Adams. Hamilton's criticism included attacks on Adams's personality, accusing the president of having an "ungovernable temper" and a "disgusting egotism." Hamilton also criticized several of Adams's policy decisions, including the pardon of the rebellious Pennsylvania farmer John Fries and Adams's position toward France. Hamilton never accused Adams of misconduct, however, and he even concluded the pamphlet with an admission that Adams had a few talents as president. Regardless, the damage was done. One prominent Federalist effectively annihilated the reputation of another on the eve of the elections. The Republicans were ecstatic, and Jefferson rejoiced in his almost certain victory. Some historians speculate that Hamilton attacked Adams out of revenge for being denied leadership in the army years earlier. Others believe Hamilton wanted to destroy the Federalist Party so he could re-create it in his own image later. Whatever Hamilton's motivation, the damage he did to Adams's public profile was catastrophic.

But there was more to Adams's defeat than the opposition of his rivals. His own policies were a handicap too. Memories of the Alien and Sedition Acts still rankled many Republicans, who thought Adams threatened the civil liberties for which the American revolutionaries had fought. While Adams never actually promoted the Alien and Sedition Acts, he let them pass without a veto. They became indelibly associated with his administration. Also, Adams's poor handling of the threat of war with France was a strong strike against him, for it managed to dissatisfy both pro-war and antiwar politicians. Adams alienated the pacifists by maintaining a strong anti-France position, referring to current relations with France as a "half-war" and refusing to pay the French minister Charles-Maurice de Talleyrand the money requested for entering trade negotiations. But Adams also alienated the war faction by unexpectedly announcing that he had nominated an emissary to the French govern-

> Adams's 1800 defeat was a historical symbol, an early lesson in American political reality.

ment—effectively suing for peace by ending the diplomatic break between France and the U.S. The Federalists were angry because Adams had seemingly caved in to a nation that threatened American business interests and because Adams had made the U.S. government appear irresolute. Republicans were pleased by the peace but perplexed as to why war talk had gone on for so long only to come to nothing. In short, no one was satisfied. Adams had tried to steer a safe course, and he deserves credit for avoiding a war that would have been devastating for a young country. But ultimately, he received little gratitude from either party. The seemingly sure tactic for winning domestic popularity—making military overtures against a perceived enemy—had not worked for Adams.

Adams's resistance to party politics was another factor in his defeat. Parties had been virtually meaningless during Washington's administration. There were no great international crises, and politicians and voters alike generally worshiped Washington. But Adams had the bad luck of holding office during a time of national self-questioning, when both foreign and domestic policy questions were fiercely debated. The differences between the Federalists and the Republicans began to matter deeply. The opposing groups solidified into a two-party system that became part of American political life, for better or worse.

Washington, for one, lamented the new importance of parties. In his farewell address before Adams's inauguration, Washington criticized the "baneful" effects of the emerging political parties. Washington's words could serve as a prophecy of Adams's presidential career, since Adams suffered the ill effects of the party system by imagining that he could remain aloof from it, as Washington had. Adams leaned toward the Federalists but was reluctant to associate himself formally with the Federalist Party. He believed that a president should reflect the interests of all citizens and shouldn't be tied to any single camp.

Adams's faith in acting as an individual rather than as a party spokesman may have been noble. But as McCullough points out, it got Adams into trouble toward the end of his term. Rather than side with Federalists and support the war against France, Adams decided to reconcile with the French by unexpectedly sending an envoy to Paris. In effect, Adams declared peace on his own. The Federalists were aghast that a leader aligned with their party took such an action without their consent. Never again would the Federalists trust Adams as a member of their group.

Indeed, Adams lost the Federalist endorsement that he desperately needed in the 1800 elections.

In a way, Adams's defeat in 1800 was a historical symbol, an early lesson in American political reality. This lesson had never been taught before, for Adams was the first incumbent president to lose in the history of America. He had no historical models to follow, so he forged ahead blindly. The unpopularity of Adams's Alien and Sedition Acts taught another lesson—that even the appearance of behaving in a monarchical way with regard to the liberties of Americans was perilous. Adams's loss of a sizable voter bloc to Aaron Burr was a lesson about the importance of aggressive campaigning. Alexander Hamilton's treachery taught Adams and future presidents the importance of reining in former colleagues who might have bones to pick and the need to maintain constant awareness of potential rivals. Finally, Adams's misguided but noble desire to rise above party affiliations cost him the support of the Federalist Party—a group on whose support he depended for reelection.

After Adams's trial by fire, no presidential hopeful or incumbent would again harbor the fantasy that political parties could go ignored in a successful campaign. Later candidates, such as Ross Perot in the 1990s, would attempt to offer third-party alternatives to Republicans and Democrats—but only by aggressively criticizing those two parties, not by trying to rise above them as Adams did. In this way, Adams helped define American political life precisely by *failing* to win a second term.

From Pittsburgh to the Pulitzer

The prolific David McCullough is one of today's most popular and acclaimed retellers of our American past.

○   ○   ○

LIKE MANY OF HIS GENERATION who grew up during World War II, David McCullough developed an abiding interest in things American. He was born in Pittsburgh in 1933, the depths of the Great Depression, and was six when the war began and nine when the United States became involved. The American experience of war and the rise of the U.S. to global leadership afterward gave him an early, deep interest in his country.

Indeed, from the outset, McCullough's works have focused overwhelmingly on American history and culture. It's probably no accident that his best-known work before *John Adams* was his biography *Truman* — a portrait of a man who served as president while McCullough was in his early twenties. Truman stands as a symbol of the America that McCullough intimately remembers.

McCullough is often drawn to studies of the American character in times of stress, threatened by war (in Adams's case, France; in Truman's, the Cold War) or by disaster (his *Johnstown Flood* is a riveting account of a community pulling together after a catastrophe). The theme of American trials and tribulations is central to McCullough's body of work. We also see in his books an underlying interest in the interplay among social classes in the United States. *The Johnstown Flood* recounts how a few rich investors built a dam for their own profit and pleasure, endangering — and eventually wiping out — a middle-class community. *John Adams* tells the story of a middle-class man who chopped his own wood, saddled his own horse, and often felt out of place among the rich and glamorous in America and Europe. This class consciousness may tie in with McCullough's own Depression experience and his exposure to the elite in college and later in life. Whatever the explanation, there's a deeply personal feel to McCullough's historical works, as if his subject weren't just randomly chosen events but part of a heritage for which he cares deeply.

McCullough was educated first in Pittsburgh and then at Yale, where he took a degree not in history, as we might expect, but rather in English literature. This choice foreshadows McCullough's writing career, since there is a literary bent to all his books. He isn't drawn to particular subjects because of overarching theoretical questions, such as why Federalists and Republicans developed and negotiated their differences in early American politics. Instead, McCullough is interested in individual personalities, like John Adams, who intrigue him.

In an interview with his publisher, Simon and Schuster, McCullough compared John Adams to a character from Charles Dickens, and we sense that for McCullough, this remark represents a tribute to the second president. In his view, it's no insult to compare his historical subject to a fictional character from a novel—it's a sign that Adams is interesting. For McCullough, the primary thing is a vibrant character. Whether that character is fictional or historical is secondary. The page-turning appeal of *John Adams* and McCullough's other works stems in large part from this viewpoint. His books read like novels. McCullough not only knows his material but also knows how to spin an engaging tale that just happens to be historically accurate as well.

This novelistic quality is key to McCullough's widespread success. Many American historians know their subjects well, but far fewer can write about them well. And there's only a handful whose works could make it onto the *New York Times* bestseller list—and stay there for more than a year, as *John Adams* did.

But McCullough is not a typical scholarly historian. He lives quietly in the small town of West Tisbury, Massachusetts, with his wife, Rosalee Barnes McCullough. He doesn't teach and isn't affiliated with any university, even though he has no fewer than thirty-one honorary degrees to his name. McCullough is a writer, not an academic, and the popular touch in his books shows it. His gift for simplicity makes him an ideal narrator for television and documentaries. He narrated a PBS film on Napoleon, as well as a wildly popular series on the Civil War by the documentarian Ken Burns. McCullough has also hosted two television series, *Smithsonian World* and *The American Experience*. He has lectured in the White House (whose first presidential inhabitant was John Adams) in conjunction with the presidential lecture series. He's also one of the few private citizens to have spoken before a joint session of Congress.

McCullough has won a wide range of historical and literary honors. He has received the *Los Angeles Times* Book Award, the Francis Parkman Prize for history, and two Pulitzer Prizes—one for his biography of Truman, another for *John Adams*. McCullough has received the National Book Award twice, once for history and once for biography. He is a member (and has served as president) of the American Academy of Arts and Sciences, which coincidentally was founded by none other than John Adams. McCullough has received the National Book Foundation Distinguished Contribution to American Letters Award, the National Humanities Medal, the St. Louis Literary Award, the Carl Sandburg Award, and the New York Public Library Literary Lion Award. The list of honors goes on and on.

But perhaps the most meaningful recognition of all is the fact that, unlike most American writers and historians, McCullough has not seen a single one of his published works go out of print. Besides his works on Truman, Adams, and the Johnstown flood, he has met success with *Brave Companions* (1991), a series of vignettes about heroic figures from history; *Mornings on Horseback* (1981), about the young Theodore Roosevelt; *The Path Between the Seas* (1977), about the construction of the Panama Canal; and *The Great Bridge* (1972), about the efforts of the a nineteenth-century father-and-son engineering team to build the greatest bridge ever attempted, the Brooklyn Bridge. But *John Adams* is McCullough's biggest success to date. The book has sold a staggering million and a half copies in hardcover, which is almost inconceivable for a book of history. But despite the profits of *John Adams*, McCullough remains a hardworking and active writer, though he somehow manages to find time for his five children and fifteen grandchildren as well.

The New Kid on the Block

In Adams's time, America was seen — and frequently mocked — as a remote, backward outpost of little importance.

○ ○ ○

THE AMERICA OF JOHN ADAMS'S PRESIDENCY was such a vastly different nation from the one we know today that we're forced to adjust our view of it before we can appreciate Adams's achievements and career. America was not a global superpower or and was by no means impressive in economic or military terms. It was barely a nation at all, at least from the perspective of international relations: in the 1790s, very few countries in the world had diplomatic ties of any sort with the U.S. It was a distant outpost in the middle of nowhere, with little importance for Europeans of the day. The wife of a member of Parliament once made a revealing comment to Abigail Adams during Adams's stint as first U.S. ambassador to Britain. The Englishwoman naturally assumed that any American would rather live in Britain if given the choice: "But surely you prefer this country to America?" It was unthinkable to her — and to most people of culture at the time — that America was really a habitable or civilized place.

Adams endured this same lack of respect in his status as representative of the U.S. Today, the job of American ambassador to Britain is one of the most honored positions in the U.S. government — but in Adams's day, many Englishmen considered it vaguely ridiculous. The British popular press mocked Adams as a clown who lacked the wealth befitting an ambassador. They regularly labeled Americans treasonous and cowardly. Things weren't much better in the Netherlands, where it took Adams nearly six months to convince a Dutch official to speak with him about loans Adams was seeking for the young United States. In France, the foreign minister gave the American envoys only fifteen minutes to give their plea for peace.

In short, the America of Adams's time was no force to be reckoned with. It's hard for us today to imagine the way America and Americans were dismissed as insignificant or ridiculous on the international scene at the time. In light of these European attitudes of the time, Adams's diplomatic successes are even more impressive.

Moreover, America was no success story at home either. The country had a lackluster military to say the least. When Adams took office as second president, the country—incredibly—had no resources for a decent standing army and no navy to defend its lengthy coastline. (Building a navy would ultimately be one of Adams's most important contributions.)

Economically, politically, and militarily, the America of Adams's time was no force to be reckoned with.

From an economic standpoint, the view was not much rosier. At the beginning of the Adams administration, there was still no standardized national currency. Americans still traded in European coinage, even after fighting a revolution to break free from Britain. There was no federal treasury or national bank to stabilize the money supply and keep an eye on the economy.

The country could not afford a presidential salary that was appropriate, as Adams discovered to his chagrin when he moved to the expensive capital city of New York. When he later moved to the new city of Washington, D.C., he found the place a swampy, muggy, mosquito-infested dump. Abigail was distraught by their desolate new quarters. There was hardly any furniture to put in the newly built White House, few paintings to hang on the walls, and no funds to hire a suitable staff. Lacking an independent fortune himself and subject to frequent money worries, Adams was actually prepared for the fiscal strains of his nation—probably far better prepared than were Jefferson or Washington, whose vast wealth may have kept them out of touch with the nation's economic welfare.

Slavery was a brutal fact in the United States during Adams's lifetime. Adams, like many New Englanders, abhorred slavery for moral and religious reasons. But others had more mixed feelings about it. They either defended slavery outright or accepted it as a necessary evil of the U.S. economy. Of course, it was too early for Adams's generation to witness the disaster that slavery would cause. The broader consequences of slavery for the U.S. didn't arise until a few decades after Adams's death, with the rising tensions that eventually led to the Civil War.

Even so, slavery still divided the Founding Fathers in important ways as early as the 1770s. It was Jefferson who penned the famous words "All men are created equal" in the Declaration of Independence. Adams opposed adding this phrase. He believed that though all men should have equal rights before the law, they are not necessarily created or *born* equal—some are stronger, taller, or smarter than others. Jefferson's stance was dubious in the first place—he owned 200 slaves on his Virginia estate, and they were decidedly *not* equal to their master. The institution of slavery conditioned Jefferson's life thoroughly: his earliest childhood memory was of a slave carrying him on a pillow.

These contradictory attitudes toward slavery persisted for decades, finally exploding into the Civil War of the 1860s. But the rift within America on the issue would prove to be a dividing point in the American doctrine of liberty and equality for all—one that wouldn't be fully acknowledged until the civil rights movement of the 1960s.

Another contradiction in America at Adams's time was the split between noble ideas and hard facts. The American Revolution had been fought in the name of some very grand ideas. Citizens' participation in their government, freedom of speech, freedom from religious persecution, the right to liberty and the pursuit of happiness, and other ideas all emerged from English and French thinkers like John Locke and Charles de Montesquieu. Pop philosophers like Thomas Paine then spread these ideas throughout the American colonies.

In a sense, the American Revolution was an intellectual event. The Founding Fathers were proud of their contribution to the history of ideas. The Constitution makes it clear that men like Jefferson and Adams realized that the document would become an intellectual landmark. But at the same time, the blunt facts of economic and social reality in the new nation often tested America's high-minded principles. After the Revolution, some continued to believe that maintaining the American ideal was the most important concern, whereas others thought that more practical economic and military concerns were more pressing.

The split between these two ways of thinking became the main division between the Federalist and the Republican parties. The Republicans were popular in the rural and frontier regions of America, where independence was a way of life and where people cared more about their own liberty than about big business, law and order, and centralized power. The Republicans' spokesman in the 1780s and 1790s was Jefferson. The Federalists insisted on more practical priorities, such as enforcing the law of the land, maintaining order, guaranteeing trade-friendly conditions, and generally keeping a strong central government. The Federalists' spokesman—sometimes an unwilling one, since he was ambivalent about political parties—was Adams.

The clash between the Republicans and Federalists was muted during Washington's tenure, but during Adams's administration, it broke out with a vengeance. The spark was the possibility of war with the post-revolutionary regime in France. In many ways this was *the* question of the 1790s. It determined whether the young America would enter a costly and draining military engagement. Maybe more important, it revealed the conflict between idealism and pragmatism in America. Leaders who placed ideas above all else, like Jefferson, saw post-revolutionary France as a symbol of everything America stood for—the struggle for freedom from tyranny and oppression and the ideals of equality and democracy. They were mindful of the help that France had given the American colonies during the war with Britain. Jefferson and his peers couldn't bear the thought of an American war against France, even when the carnage and chaos in France at the time cast doubts on the revolutionaries' commitment to democratic ideals. On the other side were American leaders who

America the deserted

In 1800, the U.S. was a nation of just 5.3 million people, spread across sixteen states. Eighty percent of these citizens were farmers, and only five percent lived in towns of 2,500 or more. The nation's largest city was New York—a whopping metropolis of 60,000—followed by Philadelphia, Baltimore, Boston, and Charleston (South Carolina). Today, the borough of Manhattan alone is home to more than 1.5 million people—nearly nine times larger than the combined population of the five largest cities in 1800.

emphasized practical concerns and generally favored war. Indeed, French ships were aggressively blocking American sea trade with Britain, since the French saw all American contact with the British as a punishable alliance with France's mortal enemy. Adams and others believed that the damage the French attacks at sea were doing to the American economy could not go unanswered.

A Reputation Restored

In *John Adams,* McCullough revisited what many considered a boring subject and turned it into a runaway bestseller.

MCCULLOUGH ORIGINALLY PLANNED to write a parallel biography of both John Adams and Thomas Jefferson. This original intent implies that McCullough may have initially felt that Adams's life was educational primarily as a contrast to someone else's life. Perhaps at the outset McCullough felt that Adams himself might not have been interesting enough to warrant a 700-page book.

Many Americans have held similar assumptions about John Adams. Before McCullough's book appeared, many Americans who knew anything about Adams at all adhered to the way the popular Broadway play *1776* portrayed him—as a vain, self-aggrandizing, blustery, and fairly foolish man. McCullough has mentioned *1776* in interviews, saying he believes its portrait of Adams to be off the mark. His book revises Adams's reputation dramatically. By focusing on Adams exclusively, McCullough asserts that Adams is an interesting historical figure and biographical subject in his own right.

It appears that the public agrees. By the end of the summer of 2002, *John Adams* had been on the *New York Times* bestseller list for over a year and was already in its thirty-fourth printing. More than a million and a half copies had sold in hardcover, and September 2002's paperback edition also became a *New York Times* number-one bestseller. In short, McCullough's book has become a worthy and successful tribute to an

American president who has been long overshadowed by his more illus-trious colleagues.

One reason McCullough ditched Jefferson's half of the biography may have been related to his preferred research method—reviewing the Adam-ses' personal letters. Jefferson destroyed every letter in his possession, so it's difficult for historians to get a full picture of his private life. In an inter-view, McCullough described Jefferson as "cooler, more guarded" than Adams. In fact, it may be this very lack of personal material that has given us an image of Jefferson as so aloof. McCullough had much greater access to Adams's private world, since John and Abigail constantly wrote to each other, except for a few intervals of silence on John's part. And they saved their letters faith-fully. McCullough relied heavily on the Massachusetts Historical Society's monumental archive of the Adams family correspon-dence, which contains letters writ-ten between 1639 and 1889. It was

The **archive** of **Adams family correspondence** comprises no fewer than 608 reels— over **five miles** —of **microfilm**.

a huge endeavor to deal with the sheer quantity of material in this archive, which comprises no fewer than 608 reels—over five miles—of microfilm.

On top of all this research, McCullough went to great lengths to get a feel for the historical period he was writing about. For what would have been the book's section on Jefferson, McCullough actually moved to Albe-marle County, Virginia—where Jefferson lived—to get a personal under-standing of the third president's surroundings. Then, to grasp the full experience of Adams's diplomatic service in Europe, McCullough and his wife, Rosalee, visited all the countries where Adams had been posted—England, France, and the Netherlands. They retraced Adams's steps pre-cisely, staying in the same villages and visiting the same monuments. They even reconstructed a tour that Adams took of some English gardens, going so far as to make sure they saw the flowers at exactly the same time of year that Adams did.

The result seems to justify McCullough's work. To many readers, *John Adams* is an appealingly fresh and intimate biography. It is especially so for readers who know only the textbook portrayal of Adams they learned of in school. McCullough's glimpse into Adams's everyday life and worries takes away a lot of the stuffiness associated with Adams. Indeed, many reviews of the biography praise McCullough's success in making Adams an interesting figure, restoring life to a man who had long been considered a dead subject. Adrian Marks's review of the book in *January* magazine says that McCullough "breathe[s] life" into material that, "in other hands, has the potential to be deadly boring." CNN likewise declared that McCullough "brings John Adams to life." *John Adams* is lively not simply because it provides an inner view of Adams's life, but also because the letters give us Adams's own take on his life. We read about the full span of Adams's life—from his work on the Constitution to his personal frustrations with his daughter's unfortunate choice of a husband—recounted in his own words. In many cases, we also see Abigail's responses in *her* own words.

But some critics see McCullough's reliance on letters as a drawback. They complain that the heavy focus on personal correspondence is excessive and that it comes at the expense of more in-depth historical analysis. The editors of the online history magazine *History House*, for example, say that it pains them to see one of their favorite historians "on autopilot like this." To them, the use of letters is fine in principle, but a "biography should be more than a convenient arrangement of the subject's personal correspondence." The inclusion of too many subjective statements from Adams takes space away from a more distanced discussion of his role in American history, cheating us out of "insight into how his life fit into the great drama of the founding of America."

It's fair to say, though, that many readers aren't bothered by the relative lack of in-depth historical analysis in *John Adams*. A biography can be many different things and serve many different functions. McCullough may simply have aimed to make Adams come alive as a person, not to offer a deep historical investigation. In any case, the frequent quoting of Adams's letters lets an authentic and intimate voice of the man be heard. The second president of the United States emerges from our dusty high-school history books with a vibrancy we never knew he had.

Other Books of Interest

John Adams isn't the first of McCullough's successes — or the first bestselling biography of a Founding Father.

○　○　○

MCCULLOUGH HAS A KNACK for lively and lucid storytelling, much like a novelist whose material is historically factual rather than made up. He displays this skill brilliantly in another of his works, *The Johnstown Flood* (1968). The book is a thrilling disaster story about one of the worst tragedies to befall America in the nineteenth century—the collapse of a dam built hastily and thoughtlessly. Inspired by the greed of a few rich men, the dam was a vain project that resulted in destruction and wiped out an entire middle-class community.

Those who appreciate McCullough's way of explaining complex situations simply and understandably should check out his books on famous historical engineering projects, which are often riveting. *The Path Between the Seas* (1977) recounts a seemingly unrealistic but finally successful attempt to connect the Atlantic and Pacific by means of a canal through Panama—focusing on the political, mechanical, and personal challenges that this project entailed.

The Great Bridge (1972) is similarly technical, but it manages to bring excitement to topics like leverage and suspension cables. Its background is more human and no less interesting: a father-son team of engineers the Brooklyn Bridge, facing almost unimaginable skepticism and pessimism from the beginning stages of their project to the end. Admirers of McCullough's skill in biography can explore his Pulitzer Prize-winning *Truman*, which, like *John Adams*, restores a great deal of credibility and honor to the memory of a man who has been neglected in the sweep of history. McCullough's study of the young Theodore Roosevelt, *Mornings on Horseback* (1981), is also noteworthy.

Earlier biographies of John Adams, such as John Ferling's *John Adams* (1992), give us different perspectives on the second president than what we find in McCullough's work. A narrower and somewhat drier focus on Adams's presidency can be found in Ralph Adams Brown's *The Presidency of John Adams* (1975). Stephen G. Kurtz explores Adams's relationship with the burgeoning Federalist Party in *The Presidency of John Adams: The Collapse of Federalism, 1795–1800* (1957). Walt Brown's *John Adams and the American Press* (1995) takes a look at the fascinating topic of Adams's difficult relations with the fledgling American press. Alternatively, John R. Howe gives insight into Adams's evolution as a political thinker in *The Changing Political Thought of John Adams* (1966).

A seemingly endless series of books on the other Founding Fathers provide a wealth of information about Adams's political peers. The many interesting works on Thomas Jefferson include the highly readable biographies *American Sphinx: The Character of Thomas Jefferson* (1997) by Joseph J. Ellis, *The Lost World of Thomas Jefferson* (1948) by Daniel J. Boorstin, and *Thomas Jefferson: An Intimate History* (1974) by Fawn Brodie. Andrew Burstein's *The Inner Jefferson: Portrait of a Grieving Optimist* (1995) provides a more psychological portrait of the third president. For a defense against rumors about Jefferson's allegedly scandalous personal life, see *The Jefferson Scandals: A Rebuttal* by Virginius Dabney (1981). Finally, Lester J. Cappon explores the hot-and-cold relationship between Jefferson and Adams in *The Adams-Jefferson Letters* (1959).

Interested in George Washington? Stamina helps. One of the foremost works is the monumental three-volume biography by James Thomas Flexner: *George Washington Vol. I: The Forge of Experience, 1732–1775* (1965), *George Washington Vol. II: In the American Revolution, 1775–1783* (1967); and *George Washington Vol. III: Anguish and Farewell, 1793–1799* (1969). For more on Alexander Hamilton, see Richard Brookhiser's *Alexander Hamilton* (1999) and Marie B. Hecht's *Odd Destiny: The Life of Alexander Hamilton* (1982).

The intellectual spirit of Adams's times is a fascinating topic, for many early Americans were torn between idealistic commitment to noble values on one hand and a more practical search for economic security on the other. Henry Steele Commager's classic *Empire of Reason: How Europe Imagined and America Realized the Enlightenment* (1977) explores the philosophical meaning of American independence. Another interesting study of the ideas behind the American Revolution is Benson Bobrick's *Angel in the Whirlwind: The Triumph of the American Revolution* (1997). A less theoretical social history of the period can be found in *A Restless People: Americans in Rebellion, 1770–1787* (1982) by Oscar and Lilian Handlin.